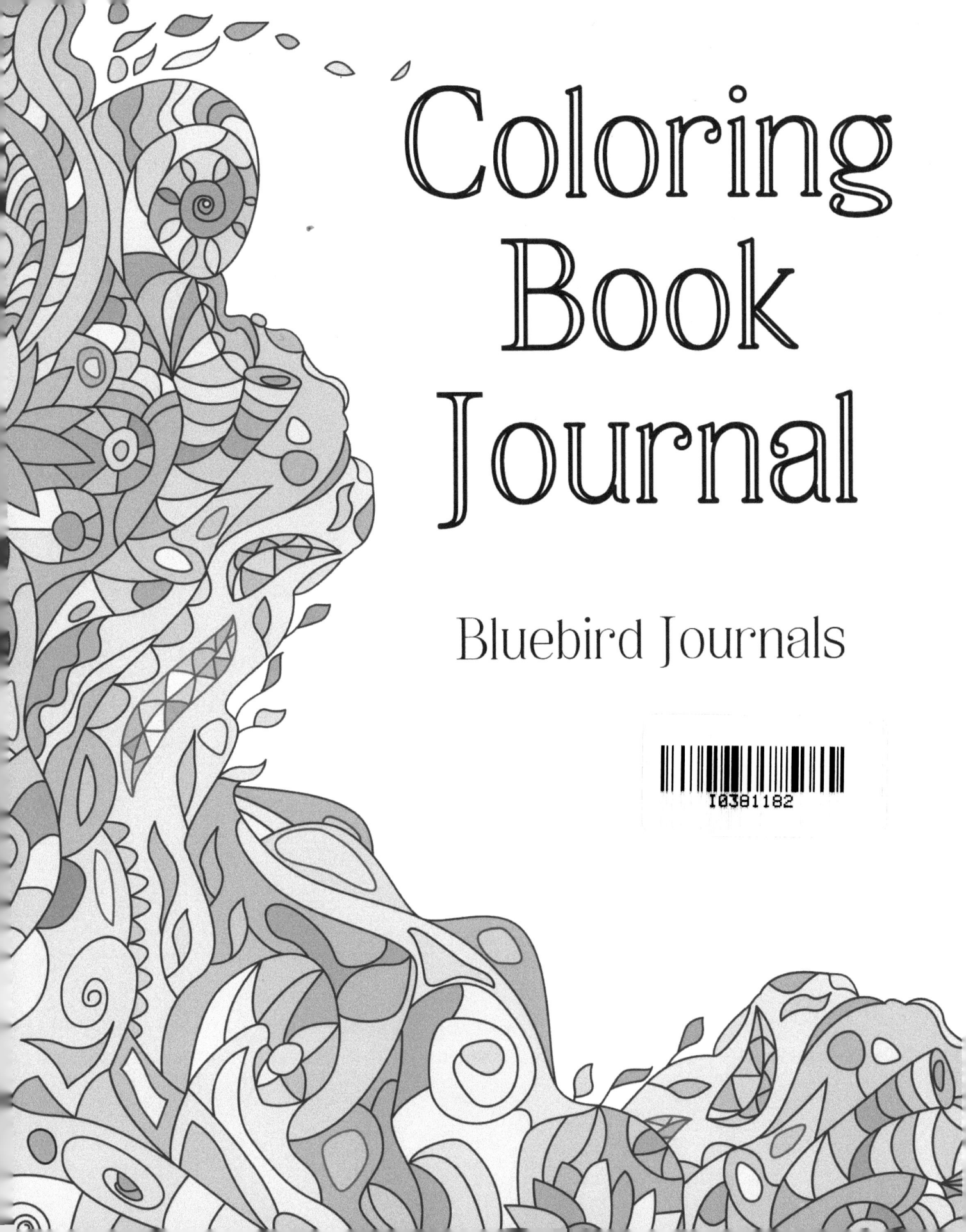
# Coloring Book Journal

Bluebird Journals

My thoughts for today...

*My thoughts for today…*

_____
_____
_____
_____
_____
_____
_____
_____
_____
_____

My thoughts for today...

_____
_____
_____
_____
_____
_____
_____
_____
_____

My thoughts for today...

_____
_____
_____
_____
_____
_____
_____
_____
_____
_____

*My thoughts for today…*

_____
_____
_____
_____
_____
_____
_____
_____
_____

*My thoughts for today...*

_____
_____
_____
_____
_____
_____
_____
_____
_____

My thoughts for today...

_____
_____
_____
_____
_____
_____
_____
_____
_____
_____

My thoughts for today...

*My thoughts for today . . .*

_____
_____
_____
_____
_____
_____
_____
_____

My thoughts for today...

_____
_____
_____
_____
_____
_____
_____
_____
_____
_____

My thoughts for today...

_____
_____
_____
_____
_____
_____
_____
_____
_____
_____

My thoughts for today...

_____
_____
_____
_____
_____
_____
_____
_____
_____
_____

My thoughts for today...

_____
_____
_____
_____
_____
_____
_____
_____

My thoughts for today...

_____
_____
_____
_____
_____
_____
_____
_____
_____
_____

My thoughts for today...

_____
_____
_____
_____
_____
_____
_____
_____
_____
_____

*My thoughts for today...*

_____
_____
_____
_____
_____
_____
_____
_____
_____

*My thoughts for today...*

_____
_____
_____
_____
_____
_____
_____
_____

*My thoughts for today...*

_____
_____
_____
_____
_____
_____
_____
_____
_____

My thoughts for today...

_____
_____
_____
_____
_____
_____
_____
_____
_____

*My thoughts for today . . .*

_____
_____
_____
_____
_____
_____
_____
_____
_____
_____

*My thoughts for today…*

_____
_____
_____
_____
_____
_____
_____
_____
_____
_____

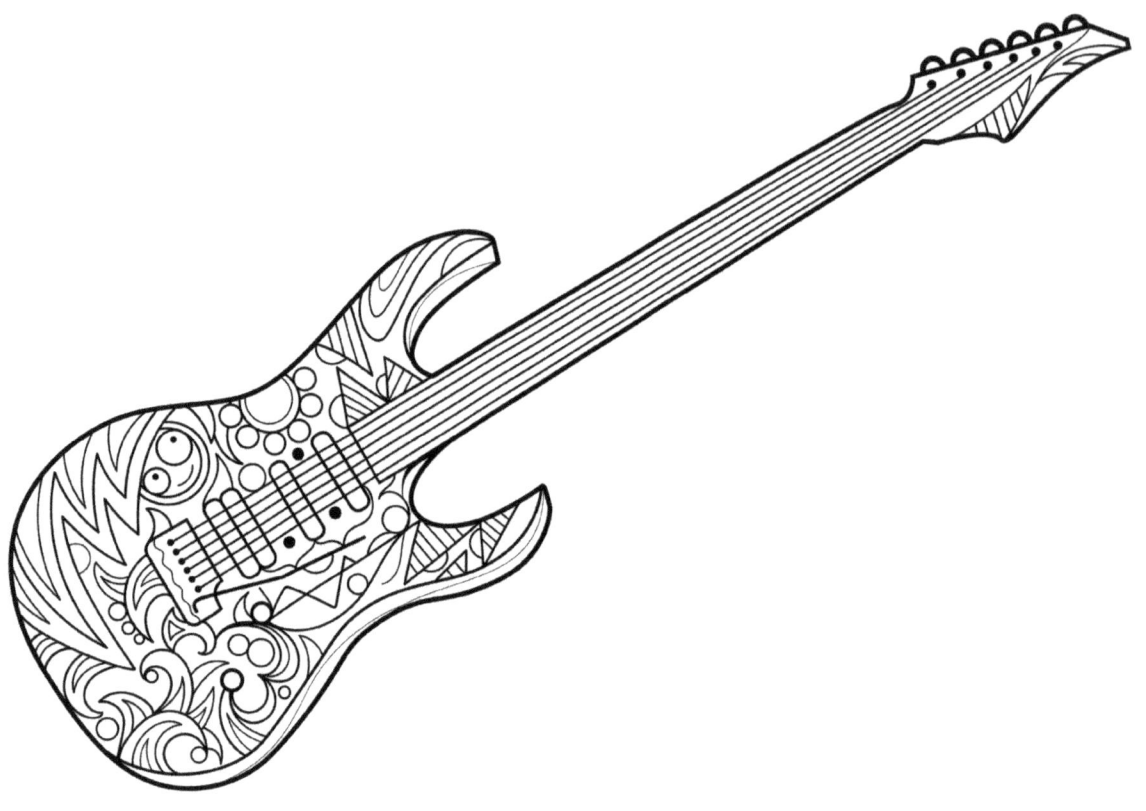

*My thoughts for today . . .*

_____
_____
_____
_____
_____
_____
_____
_____
_____
_____

My thoughts for today...

_____
_____
_____
_____
_____
_____
_____
_____
_____

*My thoughts for today…*

_____
_____
_____
_____
_____
_____
_____
_____
_____

My thoughts for today...

_____
_____
_____
_____
_____
_____
_____
_____
_____

*My thoughts for today...*

_____
_____
_____
_____
_____
_____
_____
_____
_____

*My thoughts for today . . .*

_____
_____
_____
_____
_____
_____
_____
_____
_____

My thoughts for today...

_____
_____
_____
_____
_____
_____
_____
_____
_____
_____

My thoughts for today…

_____
_____
_____
_____
_____
_____
_____
_____
_____

My thoughts for today...

_____
_____
_____
_____
_____
_____
_____
_____
_____
_____

My thoughts for today...

_____
_____
_____
_____
_____
_____
_____
_____
_____
_____

My thoughts for today...

_____
_____
_____
_____
_____
_____
_____
_____
_____
_____

My thoughts for today...

_____
_____
_____
_____
_____
_____
_____
_____
_____

My thoughts for today...

_____
_____
_____
_____
_____
_____
_____
_____
_____
_____

*My thoughts for today…*

_____
_____
_____
_____
_____
_____
_____
_____
_____
_____

*My thoughts for today...*

_____
_____
_____
_____
_____
_____
_____
_____
_____
_____

My thoughts for today...

*My thoughts for today...*

My thoughts for today...

_____
_____
_____
_____
_____
_____
_____
_____
_____
_____

*My thoughts for today...*

_____
_____
_____
_____
_____
_____
_____
_____
_____
_____

*My thoughts for today...*

My thoughts for today...

_____
_____
_____
_____
_____
_____
_____
_____
_____

My thoughts for today...

_____
_____
_____
_____
_____
_____
_____
_____
_____
_____

My thoughts for today...

_____
_____
_____
_____
_____
_____
_____
_____
_____

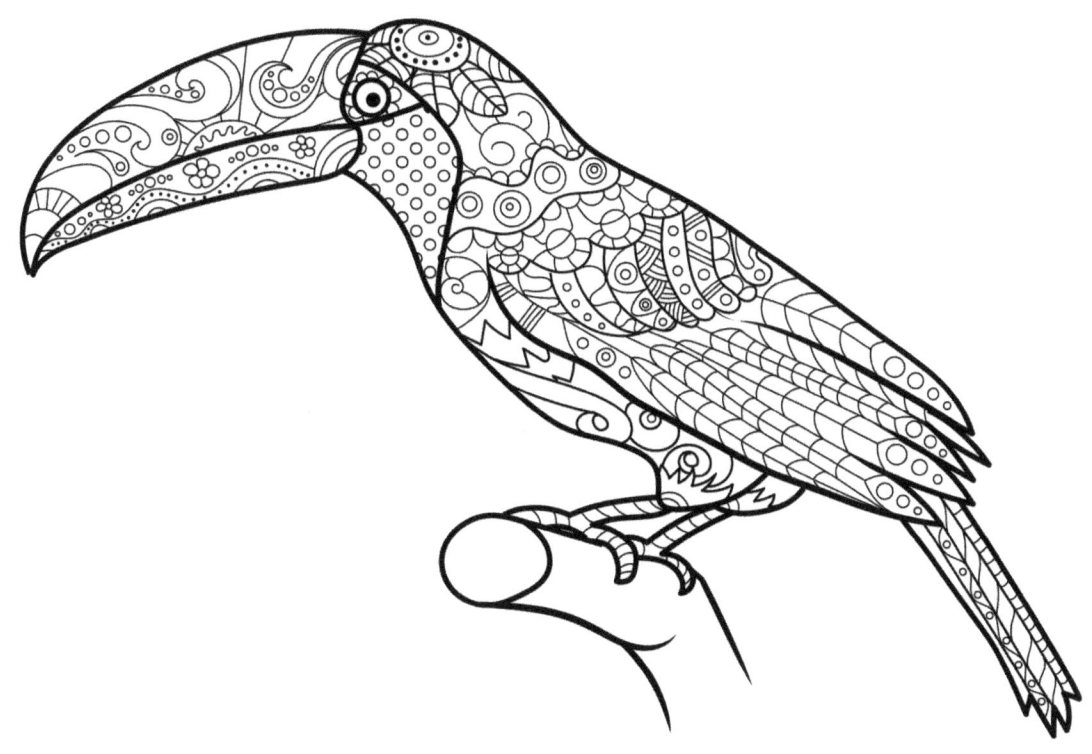

*My thoughts for today...*

_____
_____
_____
_____
_____
_____
_____
_____

*My thoughts for today . . .*

_____
_____
_____
_____
_____
_____
_____
_____

My thoughts for today...

_____
_____
_____
_____
_____
_____
_____
_____
_____

My thoughts for today...

_____
_____
_____
_____
_____
_____
_____
_____
_____

*My thoughts for today…*

_____
_____
_____
_____
_____
_____
_____
_____
_____

*My thoughts for today . . .*

_____
_____
_____
_____
_____
_____
_____
_____
_____

*My thoughts for today . . .*

_____
_____
_____
_____
_____
_____
_____
_____
_____
_____

*My thoughts for today...*

*My thoughts for today…*

_____
_____
_____
_____
_____
_____
_____
_____
_____

My thoughts for today...

_____
_____
_____
_____
_____
_____
_____
_____
_____

*My thoughts for today…*

_____
_____
_____
_____
_____
_____
_____
_____
_____

*My thoughts for today . . .*

_____
_____
_____
_____
_____
_____
_____
_____

My thoughts for today...

_____
_____
_____
_____
_____
_____
_____
_____
_____
_____

My thoughts for today...

*My thoughts for today...*

My thoughts for today...

_____
_____
_____
_____
_____
_____
_____
_____
_____
_____

www.ingramcontent.com/pod-product-compliance
Lightning Source LLC
Chambersburg PA
CBHW051355110526
44592CB00024B/2986